NO MONEY DOWN INTERNET BUSINESS

How to build a successful online business, without spending one penny!

JOHN LAGOUDAKIS

LEGAL DISCLAIMER / LEGAL NOTICES

CONTENTS

INTRODUCTION

No Money Down Internet Business is literally a guide that will show you step-by-step how to create a successful online business, without it costing you even one penny!

I've written this book to help those out there that want to get started with having their own online business but that want to test the waters before jumping in. Those that want to give it a good go before investing any capital into it.

I've also written it for the many people out there that are just plain struggling and don't have any money to invest in an online business.

Having said that, it doesn't mean that the material covered in this book can not be used as the basis of a super successful online business on its own. It certainly can!

Who am I?

My name is John Lagoudakis and I've been making a full-time income online since 2008. I'm a father of three young children. My youngest child was less than a year old when I first looked into making money online.

My goal was to find a way to make a full-time income, working from home, so that I could spend more time with my family and, at the same time, provide a better lifestyle for them. The job that I was currently doing did pay well but it was stressful work and it kept me very busy.

In 2007, I stumbled across an ebook that taught a very simple concept for making money online. I gave it a go and was immediately successful! My profit wasn't anything to retire on (I made about $1.00) but I was so excited that it worked and saw the potential of it. Eight months later I was able to quit my job and have been working from home making a full-time income online ever since.

In 2009, Clickbank awarded me as one of their top 100 affiliates and featured me in the New York Times Bestseller, 'Get Rich Click' alongside other successes, including Chris Farrell.

Over the years I've learnt a lot about what works and what doesn't work. I've seen many, many 'make money online' systems come and go; some of them good, many of them total rubbish. I've also helped a lot of people get a profitable Internet business up and running and make their first sale.

This book is a great resource for anyone just starting out online and anyone can have success with it. In fact, I've written it specifically so that literally anyone can take this and use it. Unfortunately, most people don't take action. Make sure that YOU do!

Enjoy :)

1 THE THREE WAYS TO MAKE MONEY ONLINE

There are a ton of different 'make money online' systems being promoted out there. This makes it super confusing for anyone that is looking to start an Internet business.

Which one do you go with?

To help you understand better the opportunities that are available online, I'm going to break it down for you. Basically, there are three ways that you can make money online:

1. Promote Your Own Product

2. Sell Advertising Space

3. Sell Other People's Products

Let me go into detail of all three...

1. Promote Your Own Product

This is pretty self-explanatory. If you have a product you want to sell, you can sell it online. This can be a physical product (like the many products that are sold each day on eBay) or it can be a digital product (e.g. an ebook).

This book will not be looking into this option because it will cost you money to do this, which is against the purpose of this book. However, the strategies that you learn here you can use to promote your own products if you ever decide to in the future.

Also, promoting your own products is not a good way to begin your Internet business if you are a beginner, for the following reasons:

a. Very time consuming

When you're first starting out online, it's best to work on learning the skill of how to drive traffic (visitors) to your website. This is the MOST important skill. You don't need to have your own product to do this.

Creating your own product takes a lot of time and is not the best use of your time. It's like buying a Ferrari before you even begin to learn how to drive!

Once you've found a market that is hot, and you know how to drive a lot of targeted traffic to a website, and you begin making profits, then is the time that you will want to start working on creating your own product if you decide to do so.

b. Know your market first

Many people make the mistake of creating a product or service based on what they personally like. They spend a lot of time and effort on creating the product or service only then to find, many times, that there isn't much of a market for it or that they've set it up all wrong.

By promoting other people's products as an affiliate (we will talk about this in more detail later), you get to know your market. You come to know what they like and what they don't like. Also, you get to know which products are successful and how those successful products are marketed.

This experience is invaluable.

I didn't create my first product until I had been making a full-time income online for 3 and a half years, promoting other people's products. Then, when I did create mine, I knew exactly what the market wanted and how to market it.

Was it a success? Yes, it was a HUGE success!

c) Traffic is king!

No matter how good your product or service is, if you can't get it in front of enough people, you won't succeed. When you're first starting out, you typically

4

won't know how to drive quality traffic to your site. As this is the most important skill, you will need to learn how to do this first and learn how to do it well.

In the following chapters, I'll discuss the free traffic methods that I use to drive a high volume of quality, targeted traffic to my sites.

2. Sell Advertising Space

There are a lot of website owners out there that are making good money simply selling advertising space on their website. They allow other people to put text ads or banner ads on their site for a week or a month.

Website owners that sell advertising space will offer that space for different amounts, depending on the position of the ad on the page, and how much traffic they get to their site each day.

The more prominent the ad position (e.g. in the header of the page) and the more traffic your site gets, the more you can charge for advertisers to place their banners on your site.

A good example of this is the Super Bowl, the most-watched sporting event in the world. On average, 111 million Americans watch this event every year. The cost to air a 30-second TV commercial during the Super Bowl is a whopping $4 million!

To advertise on a local TV station, you can pay as little as $25 for 30 second commercial that is played in the middle of the night.

It is exactly the same on the Internet.

If your site is high-traffic, and if your target audience are in a niche that are looking to buy, then you can charge a lot of money for companies to place their banners on your website.

The way most Internet marketers make money selling advertising space on their sites is to partner up with Google Adsense. Google gives them a few lines of code that they can place on their site which allows Google to place banners on the web pages.

Here's an example of a site that has Google Adsense ads on it:

Google's programmers are very clever. Without you having to tell them anything, Google will search your site and once it knows what type of site it is (e.g. a business opportunity site, a woodworking site, etc) it will then place ads on the site that is relevant to that niche.

Site owners can earn money with Adsense based on impressions (e.g. earning $0.25 for every time an advertisement is shown 1000 times) or they can earn money for every time an advertisement is clicked on by a website visitor (e.g. $0.50 per click).

That might not sound like exciting money but think about it... some of these sites get 1,000,000 visitors every single day! If only 1 in every 100 visitors clicked on an ad, that would be 10,000 ad clicks per day. If the earning was $0.50 per click, that would equal $5,000 per day in pure profit!

That's a lot of money. But even better than that, it's passive income :)

3. Sell Other People's Products

Selling other people's products is commonly referred to as 'affiliate marketing'. This is where you earn a commission for referring sales, and the best part is it is very easy to do.

There are many times you would have bought a product online through an affiliate and not even realised it! Let me give you an example...

Whenever you've been in the market to make a significant purchase have you ever done a search for a comparison of available products? Recently my mobile phone plan expired and I wanted to make sure I was getting the best deal so I did a search on Google for 'compare mobile phone plans'.

One of the top results was a site that listed all the different mobile phone plans available and what their different features were; plan price, calls included, data included, etc. Next to each of the phone plans was a link to the company's website.

What you may not realise is that no matter which phone plan I decide to go with, the review site will earn a commission from that company.

How?

The review site owner has an affiliate agreement with each of these phone companies. For every new customer that they refer, the website owner earns a commission. This could be a flat commission or a recurring commission.

You might be wondering how the different phone companies can know which affiliate is sending them new customers. This will be discussed in greater detail in the next chapter.

But before we go there, let me explain to you why affiliate marketing is the best way to get started out making money online...

a) No capital required

Because you're selling other people's products, you don't need to carry inventory at all. Whether you're promoting someone's digital or physical product, you don't need to purchase it in advance and then resell it. The vendor takes care of all of that for you!

All you need to do is to use your unique affiliate link to send visitors to the offer :)

b) Don't need a website

This is a big reason why most people never go into an online business. They think that they need a website and don't know how set one up.

The great news is that you don't need a website to make money online! You don't even need to know anything about how websites work, website programming etc (though it does help).

In fact, there are some very successful Internet marketers that I know that don't know how to write one line of code!

c) Never stuck with unwanted stock

If you've ever run a physical business you'll know what I'm talking about. When you buy products to resell, or if you have created your own product, you can be left with stock that you're not able to sell. Stock that you had to pay for or spend your valuable time creating.

Affiliates never have to worry about any of that!

d) Easily move from one offer to another

Let's say you're promoting a product, as an affiliate, and you find a similar or superior product in your chosen niche that is much more profitable. You can easily switch to promoting the new product and not have to worry about the old product anymore.

e) Sell as many relevant offers as you like

As an affiliate you don't have to restrict yourself to promoting one or even a few products. You can promote as many relevant, quality products as you like within your chosen niche.

f) Don't waste time on product creation, sales letters, merchant accounts, etc

The biggest benefit of affiliate marketing is that you don't have to spend ANY time at all on coming up with a product or service to sell, creating that product, the sales letter, the download pages, product support, merchant facilities for purchasing, refunds, etc.

Most people don't realise that there is a LOT involved in selling your own products.

Out of the three methods discussed in this chapter on how to make money online, the best, easiest and cheapest way to get started is the third option, selling other people's products.

In the coming chapters I'm going to show you how to quickly and easily get your own online affiliate marketing business up and running from scratch, without it costing you a cent!

2 HOW AFFILIATE MARKETING WORKS

As mentioned in the previous chapter, affiliate marketing is EVERYWHERE. You'd be surprised just how prevalent it really is. Here are some examples of affiliate websites...

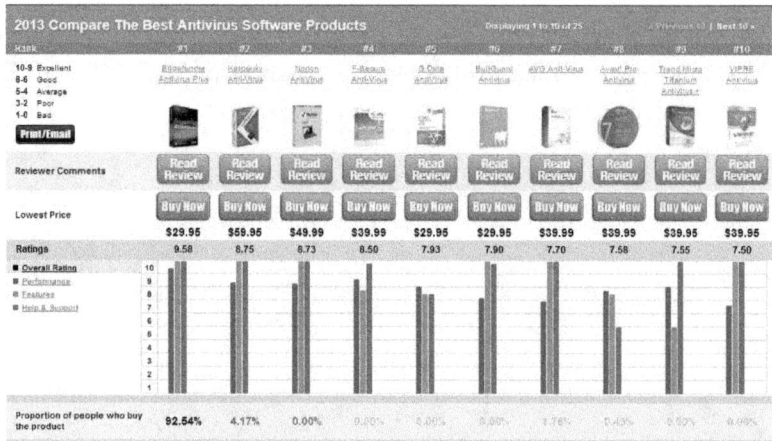

The site above came up as one of the top Google results when searching for 'antivirus software reviews'. A lot of us like to review products before we buy them, to make sure we get the best deals.

What many of us don't realise is that most of these review sites have been created with the purpose of earning money. That's not to say that the reviews are biased (that can be the case) but what it does mean is that whichever product you choose, the website owner will earn a commission.

In the example website above, the 'Buy Now' buttons take you to the antivirus' product website using this review site owner's **affiliate link**. We'll go into more details about affiliate links and how they work in Chapter 6, but for now let's just say that an affiliate link is a unique link that allows any sales to be traced back to the person that referred the sale.

For every antivirus software that is sold from visitors that have first been to the review site above, the review site owner earns a commission. Typically it is anywhere from 50 to 75% of the sale. Commissions are very high for digital products.

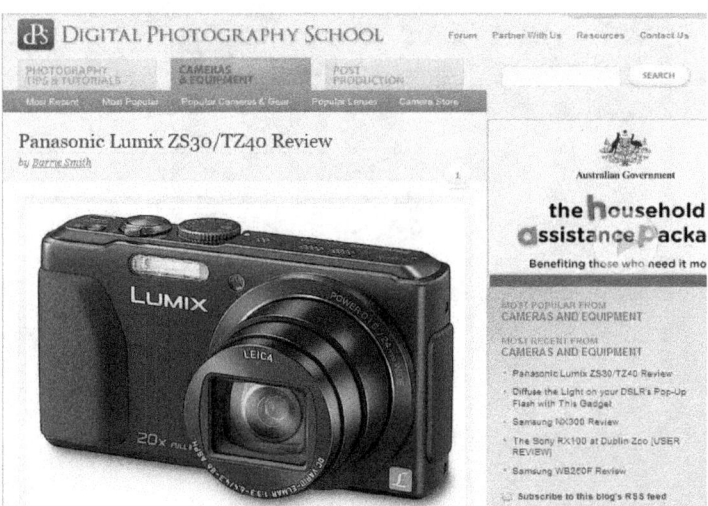

The site shown above specialises in providing information about digital cameras. Many sites that review physical products will have affiliate links going back to the product's purchase page on Amazon.com. Amazon's affiliate program pays affiliates anywhere between 4 to 15% commission on purchases referred.

The affiliate commission percentage on physical products is much lower. This is because there are much higher overheads for physical products, including product creation, delivery and support.

However, when you consider that there are literally millions of different physical products out there, and that some of these physical products sell for a lot of money, it is still a great opportunity.

Let's say you only earn 4% commissions for billiard tables. If you sell one billiard table for $15,000, your commission would be $600. That's a lot of money, especially if you never had to purchase it as a reseller in the first place, nor have to do any of the shipping, etc.

Here's another example of a typical affiliate site...

The blog above is typical of the type of site that takes you through the 'before and after' story about how someone was able to achieve something important. In this case the lady in the blog was able to lose a lot of weight within just 4 months. They will then recommend a resource that they followed to help them to achieve their goal.

Of course, there will be a link to this resource on the site...

...and, yes, that link will typically be an affiliate link.

These 'before and after' stories are particular compelling and make very good money for their owners. It works so well, that many affiliates began to create a lot of these sites but, unfortunately, many of them were making false and misleading claims.

It got so bad that the Federal Trade Commission in the U.S. (FTC) released new guidelines that came into effect in 2009. These guidelines require that affiliate sites clearly indicate that they will be receiving compensation on any purchases made from products they recommend.

The guidelines also require you to state the average result of your product or service, particularly if you are using testimonials. For example, if you have a testimonial on your site about Bob, who was able to lose 20 pounds in just 6 weeks, but the typical user of the product only loses 4 pounds over 6 weeks, you have to make a disclaimer that Bob's results are not typical.

Now that you know what affiliate marketing is, in the next chapters we're going to go into the mechanics of how it all works. Don't worry, this is easy stuff!

3 SETTING UP YOUR CLICKBANK ACCOUNT

To best help you understand just how affiliate marketing works in the Internet marketing world, we are going to set up an account on Clickbank (the biggest digital affiliate marketplace in the world), pick a product to promote, get our unique affiliate link and then make money by promoting our product.

First of all, signing up for Clickbank is very easy, quick and totally free! To get started go to their website:

http://www.clickbank.com

Once you're there, click on the 'Signup' link on the top left menu bar (see image below - don't worry if the page is not exactly as the image below, they do change their site often!).

Next, you'll see a page something like the one below. We want to sign up as an Affiliate. Clickbank currently has an offer where they will give you a whole bunch of affiliate tools for $27 a month.

While these tools may be awesome, this book is about getting you started online without spending a cent, so we are going to stick to the free affiliate account.

To get started with a free Clickbank affiliate account, select the 'I Have An Established Audience' option (see below). Yes, I know that you don't have an established audience, but that's totally okay :). If you were to select the other option, Clickbank will just try to sell you on the $27 package.

Once you reach the next page, scroll right down to the bottom until you see the 'Sign Up Now' button (see image below). Click on this button to proceed.

READY TO GET STARTED?

If you've already got an established audience, then you're ready to go! ClickBank for Affiliates lets you start earning money from your site—quickly. And it's *Free!*

Next, you will see a page where you can enter your information (see below).

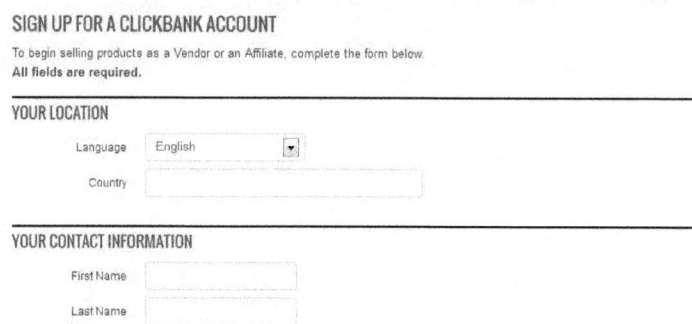

After you've entered all the information, submit the form by clicking on the 'Submit Account Registration' button (see below).

Note: The 'I have read and agree to the terms and conditions' checkbox will be disabled unless you scroll all the way down to the end of the Client Contract.

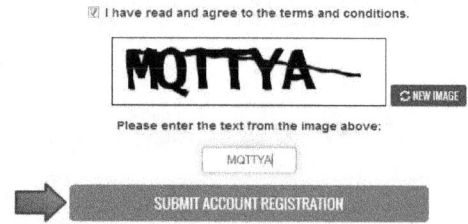

If you've filled in the Clickbank account form correctly, your submission will go through and you'll be taken immediately into the membership area of your new Clickbank account! (see below)

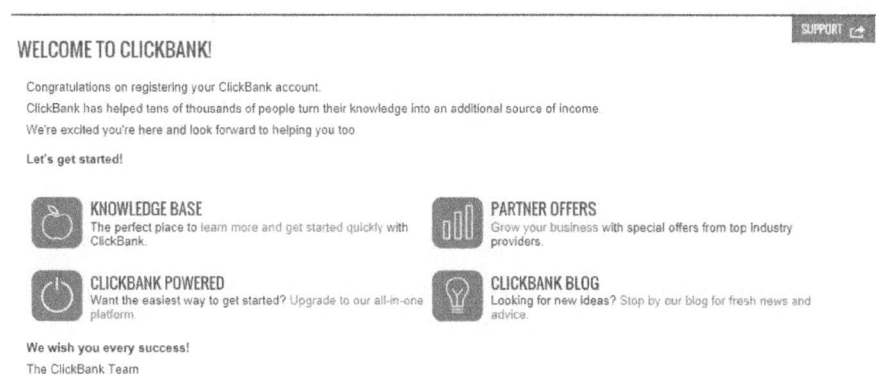

If you scroll down the page a little, you'll see something like this:

Congratulations! You've just created an affiliate account on the biggest digital marketplace in the world. But here's the exciting part...

As you start making sales as an affiliate marketer, you will see your earnings appear in your membership area (in real time!) under 'Weekly Sales Snapshot' and 'Daily Sales Snapshot'.

For that to happen, we need to take the first step. That first step is selecting which product, of the many thousands, to promote.

4 CHOOSING A GREAT PRODUCT TO PROMOTE

Choosing which products your going to promote online is crucial to your success.

Let me repeat that. **Choosing which products your going to promote online is crucial to your success.**

It takes a considerable amount of effort to promote products online (or offline) so you want to make sure you're not wasting your time. Let me give you an example of what I'm talking about here. Two friends, Bob and Pete, decide to each open their own business...

Bob does his research and decides to open a food and beverage diner on a highly trafficked area in the middle of a dessert on a stretch of road that has no competitors for many miles.

Pete loves old music and decides to open a vinyl record store.

Whose business is going to be more profitable? Bob's will, of course!

Okay, that's an extreme example but I chose that to help you understand an important point. When deciding on what you're going to promote online, make sure that you're looking at what the market wants, rather than what you're interested in personally.

Many, many people make the mistake of going into business thinking that, "If I like this, everyone else will like it too!" That is not always the case.

I'm not saying that you should promote products purely based on how hot the market is. It is best if you find a niche that you're also passionate about. This greatly helps motivate you in your business. What I am saying is that you should never lose sight of the fact that you are in business to provide a valuable service and to make a profit.

Anything else is not a business. It's a hobby.

This section is dedicated to making sure that you find a great product to promote. The great news is, with so many products to choose from on the Clickbank Marketplace, you should be able to find something that you have an interest in and that will also sell well.

What I love about Clickbank is that they give you all the statistical data you need to know which products are selling well and which ones are not.

Okay, let's go to the Clickbank Marketplace right now and check it out!

While still logged into your Clickbank member's area, click on the Marketplace link in the top menu bar (see image below).

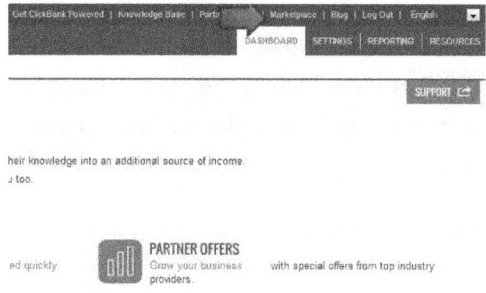

The next page you see will look something like the one below. Click on the 'Advanced Search' link near the top right of the page (see below).

On the 'Advanced Search' page there are a lot of different search options. The one that is the most important, which we will spend a little time discussing here right now, is **Gravity**.

Every product on the Clickbank Marketplace is assigned a gravity. The gravity of a product is updated daily and can range anywhere from 0 to 600 or more.

Gravity refers to **how many affiliate marketers right now are making sales of that product**.

For example, if a product has a gravity of 120, that means that right now there are 120 different affiliates out there that have made sales of that product.

Why is this important to you and me?

A high gravity is a sure sign of a great product to promote! Think about it. The more affiliates that promote a product, the better it must be. Affiliates don't spend time, effort and money promoting products that don't sell well and that are not of a good quality.

A good place to start, when looking at the gravity of a good product, is 50. Any product on the Clickbank Marketplace that has a gravity of 50 or more is sure to be a winner!

So, here at our Advanced Search page, what we want to do is go to the Gravity section, tick that checkbox, select 'Higher than' from the drop-down list and then type in 50 (see below). Once you've done this, click on the red 'Search' button.

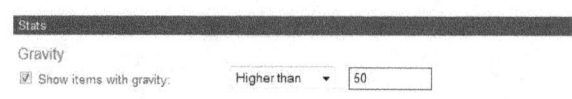

Here's what happens next...

Clickbank scanned their entire database of tens of thousands of products, and brings you back only those products that have a gravity of 50 or more. At the time that I did this search, it came back with 101 results (see image below).

This means that right now (results are updated daily) there are 101 products in the Clickbank Marketplace that have a gravity of 50 or more. That's a lot of solid products that you and I can promote. What's even better, we've eliminated tens of thousands of products that would have wasted our time!

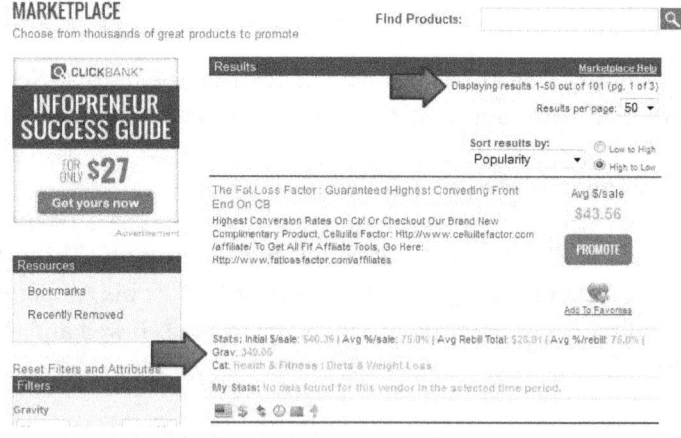

In the image above, I've included the first result of the products that came back in the search results. This particular product is called 'The Fat Loss Factor' and it has a gravity of 349. This means that 349 different affiliates are currently making sales of this product. This would be a great product to promote.

This product is in the category of 'Diets & Weight Loss'. If this is something that you're passionate about then this may be the product you will want to choose to promote. If this is not something you are interested in, I'd recommend that you go over the rest of the search results and find something that is.

For the purpose of this exercise, we are going to continue discussing this particular product.

You'll notice that Clickbank gives you a lot of feedback about each product. Important things to look out for are:

- Avg $/sale
- Is this a recurring billing product? If so, what is the Avg Rebill Total?

I'll go over each of these in a little detail.

Avg $/sale

This figure refers to how much you will earn, on average, for every initial sale that you make of this product. In the case of The Fat Loss Factor, the Avg $/sale is $43.56.

You will also notice that the percentage of the sale that is your commission is a massive 75%. The reason your commission is so large is because The Fat Loss Factor is a digital product. The cost to create digital products is much less than physical products, and the overheads (including product delivery) are very low.

This is why I enjoy promoting digital products :)

Recurring billing product

Recurring billing products are products that are a regular subscription, usually monthly but sometimes weekly or yearly. For example, on Clickbank there is antivirus software for sale that comes with a yearly subscription. If you make the initial sale, you receive your commission immediately for that initial sale, and here's the best part...

...12 months later, when the yearly subscription is paid, you will receive your hefty commission automatically!

Even today, I receive monthly commissions for sales that I initially made over 4 years ago! There's nothing better than having a consistent flow of passive commissions.

You can tell if a Clickbank product offers a recurring billing product if it has an icon of two blue arrows (see image below) and also if it has an 'Avg Rebill Total' amount:

The amount shown in the 'Avg Rebill Total' is the commission you receive on each payment cycle. In the case of The Fat Loss Factor, the recurring billing is monthly and you receive $28.91 every month for each recurring billing client you sign up.

All in all, The Fat Loss Factor is definitely a GREAT product to promote. Firstly, you have an army of affiliates already promoting it, which means that it converts super well.

Secondly, this is a HOT, evergreen niche. Weight loss has been a hot market for as long as products have been sold and will continue to be forever.

Thirdly, your commissions are substantial; $43.56 for the initial sale and $28.91 per monthly rebill (75% commissions!).

In the next chapter, we're going to look at the income potential of promoting a product like The Fat Loss Factor.

5 SHOW ME THE MONEY!

Okay, here's what it's all about. Profits!

This chapter is going to focus on how much you can expect to earn from your Internet business. We're going to go over a couple of different scenarios; Sally, a stay-at-home mom that can work on her Internet business on only a part-time basis, and Bob, a budding full-time Internet marketer.

Let's start with Sally. Sally can devote about 10 hours per week to her Internet business. She has decided to promote The Fat Loss Factor as an affiliate and is able to sign up 20 people every month.

Here's what Sally's income will look like after one year:

20 sales per month x 12 months = 240 sales

240 sales x $43.56 = $10,454.40

That means Sally has earned a total of $10,454.40 over one year on the **initial sale** of The Fat Loss Factor. This is not a bad little part-time income **but** when you factor in the recurring billing, you will see how it will make a huge difference to your business...

So let's say that of those 240 people that purchased The Fat Loss Factor, each month 5 of the 20 new buyers decide to join the monthly subscription.

That will mean that, by the end of the first year, Sally will have also earned the following recurring billing income:

5 x 11 months = 55 recurring billing payments

(for those that joined in the first month and continued to pay all year)

5 x 10 months = 50 recurring billing payments

(for those that joined in the second month and continued to pay all year)

5 x 9 months = 45 recurring billing payments

(for those that joined in the third month and continued to pay all year)

5 x 8 months = 40 recurring billing payments

(I think you get the idea now...)

5 x 7 months = 35 recurring billing payments

5 x 6 months = 30 recurring billing payments

5 x 5 months = 25 recurring billing payments

5 x 4 months = 20 recurring billing payments

5 x 3 months = 15 recurring billing payments

5 x 2 months = 10 recurring billing payments

5 x 1 months = 5 recurring billing payments

Total recurring billing payments for the year = 55 + 50 + 45 + 40 + 35 + 30 + 25 + 20 +15 + 10 + 5 = 330 recurring billing payments

Total recurring billing income for the year = 330 payments x \$28.91 = **\$9,540.30**

That means that Sally almost doubled her income just because she chose to promote a recurring billing product!

And even better than that, after one year Sally has 60 people (the 5 people that signed up to the recurring billing product every month over the past year) that are on a subscription that she is receiving income for... on **total autopilot!** That means Sally is receiving **$1,734.60** (60 x $28.91) in commissions every single month, even if she decides to not get out of bed in the morning!

Okay, let's see what Bob is doing...

Bob took the plunge and is working his Internet marketing business full-time now. He can devote about 40 hours per week to his Internet business. Bob also likes The Fat Loss Factor and has decided to promote it as an affiliate. Bob is able to sign up 80 people every month.

Here's what Bob's income will look like after one year:

80 sales per month x 12 months = 960 sales

960 sales x $43.56 = **$41,817.60**

That means Bob has earned a total of $41,817.60 over one year on the initial sale of The Fat Loss Factor. That's not too bad. Well done, Bob!

But wait, there's more ;)

Let's say that of those 960 people that purchased The Fat Loss Factor, each month 20 of the 80 new buyers decide to join the monthly subscription.

That will mean that, by the end of the first year, Bob will have also earned the following recurring billing income:

20 x 11 months = 220 recurring billing payments

(for those that joined in the first month and continued to pay all year)

20 x 10 months = 200 recurring billing payments

(for those that joined in the second month and continued to pay all year)

20 x 9 months = 180 recurring billing payments

(for those that joined in the third month and continued to pay all year)

20 x 8 months = 160 recurring billing payments

(I think you get the idea now...)

20 x 7 months = 140 recurring billing payments

20 x 6 months = 120 recurring billing payments

20 x 5 months = 100 recurring billing payments

20 x 4 months = 80 recurring billing payments

20 x 3 months = 60 recurring billing payments

20 x 2 months = 40 recurring billing payments

20 x 1 months = 20 recurring billing payments

Total recurring billing payments for the year = 220 + 200 + 180 + 160 + 140 + 120 + 100 + 80 +60 + 40 + 20 = 1320 recurring billing payments

Total recurring billing income for the year = 1320 payments x $28.91 = **$38,161.20**

That brings Bob's total income for the year to be $41,817.60 + $38,161.20 = **$79,978.80**

And here's what excites Bob...

He has now 240 people (the 29 people that signed up to the recurring billing product every month over the past year) that are on a subscription that he is receiving income for. That means Bob is receiving **$6,938.40** (240 x $28.91) in commissions every single month, without him needing to do a single thing!

This is the reason that I first got into Internet marketing... being able to earn a passive full-time income. Let me tell you, there's nothing better than having a great full-time income AND the time to enjoy it!

Following the strategies in his book will help you to achieve that goal.

Now, I must make an important disclaimer here; these recurring billing figures are in no way guaranteed. Some affiliates will earn more money in recurring billing signups than other affiliates. The degree of your success will depend, in a large measure, on the relationship you've developed with your buyers.

In the coming chapters, we'll talk about ways to develop a great relationship with buyers, before they even buy from you.

6 AFFILIATE LINKS

In Chapter 2 (How Affiliate Marketing Works) we first introduced the topic of affiliate links. Affiliate links are at the heart of how affiliate marketing works, and how most people make money online. In summary, an affiliate link is what identifies where a sale referral has come from, so that the referrer (affiliate) can be credited for the sale.

Within the Clickbank Marketplace there are literally thousands of products, however, you can easily get your unique affiliate link for every single one of them. The first step is to choose a product to promote.

In keeping with our previous examples, let's say we want to promote The Fat Loss Factor. To get your unique affiliate link for this product, this is what you do...

Step 1: Make sure you are logged into your Clickbank account.

Step 2: Go to the Clickbank Marketplace.

Step 3: Find your product in the marketplace.

If you already know which product you want to locate, a quick way to find it is to type the name of the product in the **Find Products** field (see below) and click on the search button.

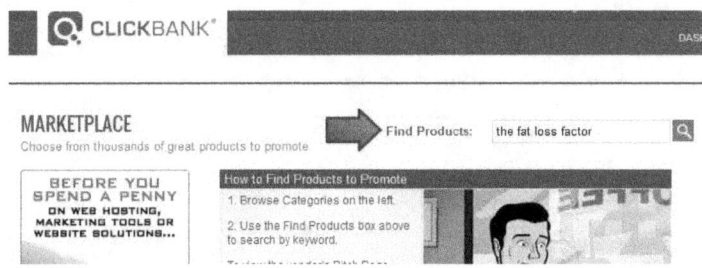

Step 4: When the search results appear, locate the product you want to promote, and click on the red **Promote** button (see below):

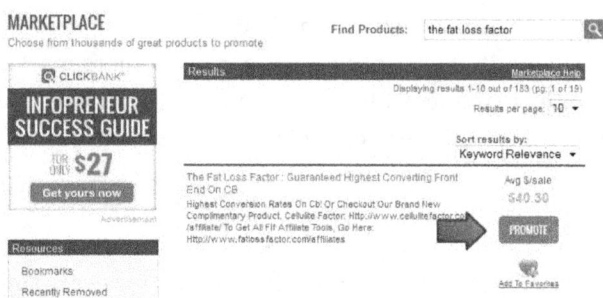

A new window will appear (see below).

Step 5: Click on the **Create** button and Clickbank will create your unique Fat Loss Factor affiliate link for you.

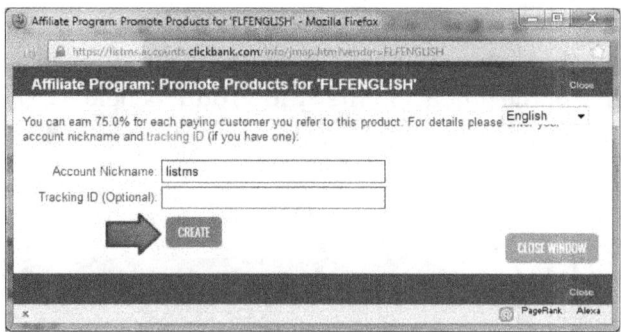

Step 6: Test that your affiliate link works correctly.

Your affiliate link will look something like this:

http://e2c179kn4g6x5pddpesihfkgmr.hop.clickbank.net

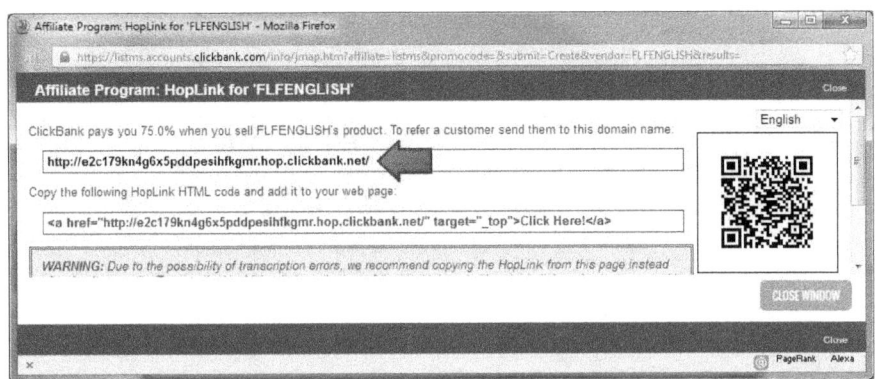

Now, if you click on this link, you'll be taken to The Fat Loss Factor sales page:

http://www.fatlossfactor.com/new/

And here's the beautiful part... whenever someone goes to The Fat Loss Factor sales page via my affiliate link and decide to buy this product, I will earn a commission! :)

Each Clickbank product's sales page will have buy button. Some of them will say '**Yes! Add To My Order**' (see example below), '**Add to Cart**', etc.

When a potential buyer clicks on the buy button, they are taken to the Clickbank checkout page for that product. Here is the Clickbank checkout page for The Fat Loss Factor:

At the bottom of the checkout page there is a line that reads [**affiliate** = *clickbank id*] (see above).

This is how you can know if your Clickbank affiliate link is working correctly. When you use your affiliate link to go to a Clickbank product's sales page and then, from there, click through to the checkout page, your Clickbank id should be shown at the bottom of the page.

If you test your Clickbank affiliate link, and then see your Clickbank id at the bottom of the checkout page, then you've done it correctly and are ready to move to the next step!

What is the next step?

The next step is getting your affiliate link in front of as many people as possible.

This doesn't mean that we are going to spam the world with our affiliate links! No, this never works out well. What you need to do is get your affiliate link in front of as many people as you can that are **interested in the product that you are promoting**.

The remainder of this book will be dedicated to helping you learn different ways to promote your affiliate offer... and best of all, every method we go over is absolutely free!

But before we start promoting your affiliate link all over the Internet, there's one more important thing we need to do, and it's related to your affiliate link. You see, there is a little problem with Clickbank affiliate links and you might have already guessed what that is...

They are so long and ugly!!!

http://e2c179kn4g6x5pddpesihfkgmr.hop.clickbank.net

Ughhh!

I mean, it's not very inviting to put a long link like that in front of someone and say, "Hey! Trust me ;) Click on this!"

So how do we get around this?

There are free services out there that allow us to 'beautify' long, ugly urls by shortening them. They are called URL shorteners and you've most probably seen them before. An example of where they are used is Twitter.

Because Twitter posts are limited to 140 characters, when someone posts something on Twitter and also includes a link, it is usually shortened (see below).

You also see this happening on Facebook...

Creating a shortened url for your affiliate link is super easy! To more clearly explain how url shortening works, let's go to a free url shortening service...

Step 1: Go to http://tinyurl.com

Step 2: Copy your Clickbank affiliate link into the field provided. If you want to, you can specify a 'Custom alias'. If this is left blank, TinyURL will generate a link for you with random letters and numbers. When you're ready, click on the '**Make TinyURL!**' button (see below).

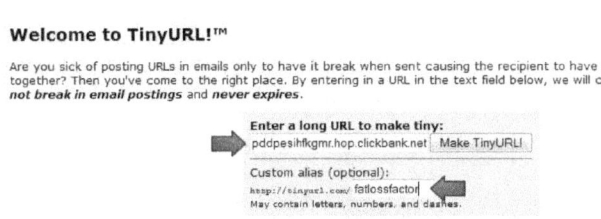

Step 3: Tada! You already have your shortened affiliate link!

In this case, TinyURL has turned my long Clickbank affiliate link for The Fat Loss Factor into this:

http://tinyurl.com/qf4r68q

(see below)

It's much better looking than that long Clickbank affiliate link, isn't it?

Now, if someone goes to http://tinyurl.com/qf4r68q, they will automatically be redirected to http://e2c179kn4g6x5pddpesihfkgmr.hop.clickbank.net ...

Which of course takes them to The Fat Loss Factor sales page :)

Okay, now that we've created our Clickbank affiliate link for the product we want to promote, and we've made it look more user-friendly, it's now time to make some money!

The remainder of this book will go over different strategies you can use to get your product in front of those that need it most... and lots of them.

7 YOUTUBE

The way that I get most of my free, targeted traffic is by far YouTube, and here's what I love about it...

YouTube is the 3rd most visited site in the world. More than 30 million unique visitors visit this site every single day, watching over 200 million hours of video each and every day!

The beautiful thing is that all this video is created by people just like you and I...

...and it's free for us to use and we can upload as many videos as we want :)

Take a look at this...

I did a search on YouTube of the Most Viewed Videos of all time. It's not surprising that most of the top 10 videos are popular music videos... but if you look below, you'll see that the 7th most viewed video of all time is a simple, 56 second home video titled "Charlie bit my finger - again!".

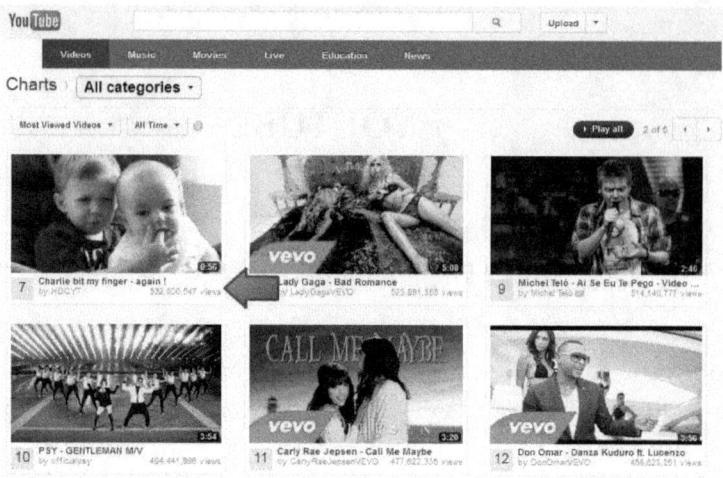

This video was uploaded by a parent and went so viral that, at the time of writing this, it has had over half a billion views!

I was so impressed by the amount of views this home video had that I decided to try my own little experiment. I took my cute young son and made a short, 6 second video where he transforms himself from Ben 10 into Humungousaur. Check out the stats below...

Can you see that.. 7,445,157 views! Not bad :)

I want you to think about this... if the person that uploaded the "Charlie bit my finger - again!" video was paid only one-tenth of 1 cent for each ad that was displayed while watching this video (you can set up your YouTube account so that ads are displayed on your videos and get paid for it), then they would have earned over **half a million dollars** from this one video alone.

Can you see the potential here?

What's even more appealing about YouTube is that the traffic you attract to you can be totally targeted. For example, if you wanted to attract visitors that were interested in losing weight, you would create videos about weight loss. It's that simple.

Now, if YouTube gets so much traffic (it's totally insane) and you use it as much as you want to for free... why wouldn't you?

A while back I made the decision to use YouTube as my main source of free, targeted traffic. So I set a goal to create 100 videos within just 5 weeks.

I went to work and did accomplish my goal. All I had to do was create 20 short, how-to videos each week over 5 weeks. That meant that I need to do 4 short videos each weekday.

Was it hard to do? Not at all! Once you've created and uploaded your first couple of videos, it is very easy to do. In this chapter I'm going to show you how.

But before I do, let me tell you the result of creating all these videos. At first there wasn't a lot of activity. I would get a few views each day on each of my videos. BUT, as time went by, my view counts began to grow exponentially.

You see, as your video is viewed and gets good feedback, YouTube promotes it more and you get more views, and it just continues to gain momentum.

At the time of writing this book, my YouTube channel has had over 700,000 views.

John Lagoudakis (johnlagoudakis)

Of those 700,000 viewers, many thousands (I estimate over 100,000) have visited my website.

And the best part is, even if I never add another video to YouTube again, I will continue to get tens of thousands of visitors to my website because of them.

How to Promote Your Affiliate Link on YouTube

Let's say you want to get lots of people on YouTube to click on your Fat Loss Factor affiliate link. How do you go about it?

It's very easy :)

YouTube allows you to display a link in the 'Description' section, just below your video. Check out one of my videos on YouTube:

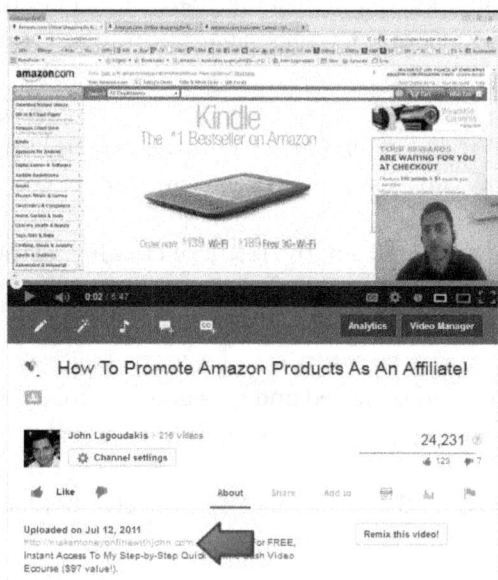

Underneath the video you can see a link to my website. Many people that watch my videos click on this link and come to my site. You can do exactly the same with your affiliate link!

What I do to increase the amount of clicks I get is to write the following after the link:

"CLICK HERE to learn more about..."

or

"CLICK HERE to discover how to..."

Here's an example of one of my video descriptions:

"CLICK HERE to discover how I quit my day job forever and work from the comfort of my own home - FREE training!"

Doing this helps your link to stand out, and you take the guesswork away from your viewers because you're telling them exactly what you would like them to do!

Once you've created your video, login to your YouTube account (YouTube accounts are free to create if you don't already have one) and click on the '**Upload**' button (see below):

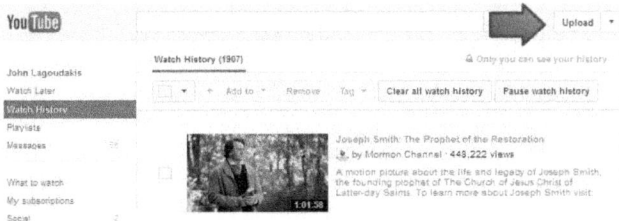

Next you will see the page below. Click on '**Select files to upload**'.

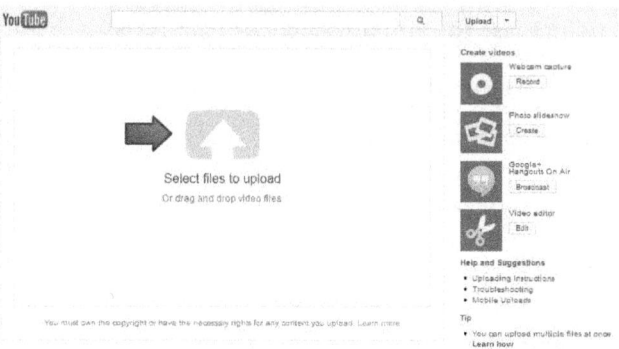

Next, browse to where your video file is, select it and click on '**Open**' (see below). Your file will then be uploaded to YouTube.

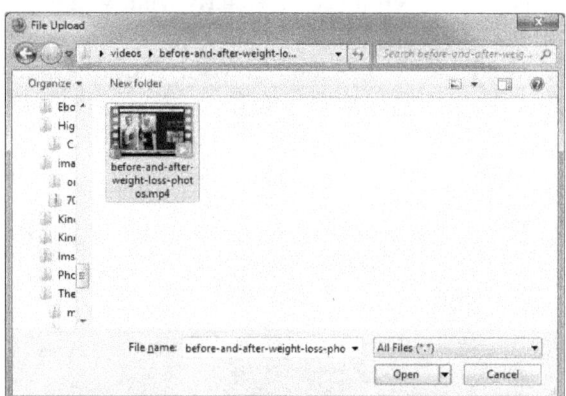

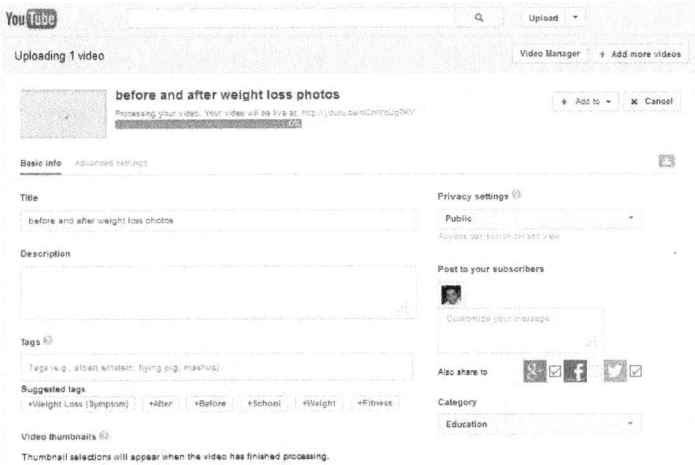

While your video is uploading and processed by YouTube (see image above), you can begin entering the information about your video.

To help promote The Fat Loss Factor, I've created a 'before and after' weight loss video. You can see below what I've entered for the Title of the video, the Description and the Tags:

The Title and the Description are seen by everyone. The tags are to help YouTube know what your video is about so they can bring it up in their search results when someone goes looking for your type of video.

The Title is very important. It should stand out and make people want to watch the video.

What we want to do with the Description is to get as many people to click on our affiliate link. That is why the link appears first in the Description and why we make it very clear what we want our YouTube viewers to do.

Here's what our new video looks like once it is live on YouTube:

And that's all there is to it! You're now have a real Internet business up and running. Congratulations!

You now have targeted visitors going to a sales page of a quality offer which you are earning 75% commission on every sale.

YouTube Marketing FAQ

The main questions and concerns I get about promoting an offer on YouTube are:

- What type of videos should I create?
- I can't offer advice... I'm not an expert!

- How do I create a video?

Let me address all of these questions.

What type of videos should you create?

First of all, you want to make sure that your video is related to your niche. If you want to attract people that are interested in weight loss, don't make a video about your favourite chocolate bars! Or even worse, a video about something totally unrelated, e.g. cars.

If you're in the weight loss niche, you'll want to create videos topics about exercise, dieting, liposuction, etc. I think you get the idea!

You'll want to keep your videos short. Don't drag on and on. Get to the point and deliver on what you promise to give. This is especially true if your video is a 'how-to' or educational video.

Videos that have worked really well for me are 'how-to' and educational videos. It's a great way to build a relationship of trust with people, by showing them how to do something.

If you want to make your video viral, i.e. get lots of views really, really fast, then you'll want to base your topic on a really hot trend or news item. E.g. a new blockbuster movie, celebrity marriage, major sporting event, etc.

Funny videos are also extremely popular and viral. If it is in your nature to make people laugh then definitely use that to your advantage.

Controversial videos also do very well. If you have a view that will really ruffle some feathers, don't be afraid to share it!

I can't offer advice... I'm not an expert!

This is a really common concern, but a totally unnecessary one.

<u>Everyone</u> has something to offer. Most of us take for granted the things that we know. You need to realise that there are things that you know, especially if you're passionate about a topic that many people don't know. You'll really be surprised.

Don't believe me? Do this; go to YouTube and do a search for videos in your niche. Now, notice how many videos there are that are teaching very basic concepts in that niche, and notice how many thousands, or millions of views those videos are getting.

That's right. There's lots of them, aren't there? The beautiful thing is that soon your video will be amongst them :)

I'll let you in on a little secret. No one is born an expert. Everyone starts from zero and works their way up. You know who the experts are? They are simply the ones that are willing to share what they know which those around them.

How do they become experts? They simply continue to teach <u>as they learn</u>, until they've learned more than what most people know. You can do exactly the same thing.

I'm considered an Internet marketing expert by thousands but just 6 years ago I knew nothing about the subject. Since that time I've learned step-by-step as I've built up my business. Along the way I taught strategies that were working for me. You can do the same.

How do I create a video?

There are three types of video you can create.

1. You can create a video of you talking in front of a camera

This is the least desired method as most people are camera shy. I remember the first videos in front of a camera that I made. I was so nervous and it showed. I cringe every time I think of those videos... I was so bad!

Looking back, though, I'm so grateful I did that and am more comfortable now in front of a camera. This is a great skill to have and allowing others to see you amplifies the relationship you can make with your visitors.

2. Screen capture videos

Screen capture videos are where you record what you see on your computer monitor. I love creating these videos for the Internet marketing niche because there is so much we do on our computers.

Examples of videos that I create are; Wordpress how-to videos (how to install plugins, write posts, etc), Clickbank how-to videos, and product reviews.

There are several free software available that will allow you to record your screen. Two that I recommend are Camstudio and Screencast-o-Matic.

3. Slideshow presentations

Slideshow videos are easy to make and are a lot of fun. You can create a slideshow of images and/or text, and then record the slideshow presentation.

It's a lot better to have audio to go along with your slideshow. This can either be you speaking about the slideshow, or you can just have background music.

You can also use Camstudio and Screencast-o-Matic to record your slideshow presentations.

In the next chapter, we are going to talk about how to use Facebook to drive lots of free, targeted traffic to our offers.

8 FACEBOOK

Facebook is now the MOST visited site in the world with over 1.1 billion members. That's an amazing achievement and for affiliate marketers it is a goldmine. Why? Because Facebook is set up so that you can create as many free pages as you like to promote your business...

...and because everyone can see, search and share everything, it's so easy to promote your products.

Some people promote affiliate offers on their Facebook personal profile. I wouldn't recommend that. Facebook profiles are meant to be social and when you start promoting items heavily it will turn people off.

How do we promote our affiliate offers on Facebook then?

Using Facebook Pages.

Some of you might be wondering, "What is a Facebook Page?" Here is the definition straight from their site:

"Pages are for businesses, organizations and brands to share their stories and connect with people. Like timelines, you can customize Pages by adding apps, posting stories, hosting events and more. Engage and grow your audience by posting regularly. People who like your Page and their friends will get updates in News Feed.

"You can create and manage a Facebook Page from your personal account."

Facebook pages are awesome. You can practically set up as many of them as you like, it's super quick and easy to do, and it's 100% free :)

How Do You Create a Facebook Page?

To create a Facebook Page, you will need to be signed in to your Facebook account. In the Search bar along the top of your Facebook page, type in the following:

"create new facebook page"

The first search result should be '**Create New Facebook Page**' (see image below). Click on this item.

Next you will be given the choice of identifying what we will be promoting on our page (see image below). Most affiliate sites will fall under the '**Brand or product**' category. We will select this for our Fat Loss Factor page.

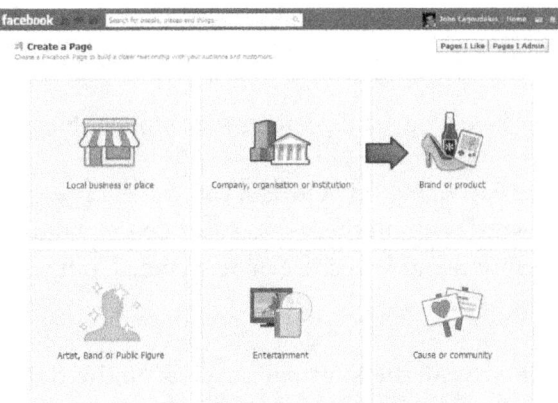

Next we will be required to select under which category our product falls. For The Fat Loss Factor we will select 'Health/Beauty'.

We also need to enter the Title of our page. This title will be seen on the page and also will be the name by which people will find it when searching online. For this product, I'm going to name the page 'The Fat Loss Factor'.

If you're happy to, tick the 'I agree to Facebook Pages Terms' checkbox and click on '**Get Started**'.

Next, we are asked to give a brief description of what our page is all about. To make things super easy, I like to head on over to the sales page of the Clickbank product I'm promoting (in this case, http://fatlossfactor.com) and copy their main headline. Headlines are very compelling, and since they've done this hard work for us, there's no need to reinvent the wheel!

Your brief description should also include a call to action to get visitors to click on your affiliate link (this is what it is all about). In the example below, I've got the words, "CLICK HERE" and then my affiliate link.

In the 'Website' field, copy and paste in your affiliate link (see below).

For your unique Facebook web address, you can enter anything you like. I prefer to separate words with dashes (-) to separate the words but you don't have to. The page Description and Website can be changed, but your unique Facebook web address cannot be.

When you've entered all the information, click on the '**Save Info**' button to continue.

If the unique Facebook web address you wanted is already taken, Facebook will ask you to try another one (see image below).

Next, you'll be asked to add a Profile Picture. You'll want to make sure you choose a picture that will really capture people's attention.

Once you have your image ready, click on '**Upload from computer**', find the image and upload it.

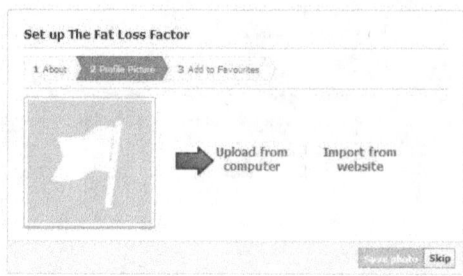

Here's the image I've selected for this page. People interested in weight loss love 'before and after' shots. They are highly motivational.

Once you've uploaded your image, you will see a preview of how it will appear on your profile. If you're happy with it, click on '**Next**'.

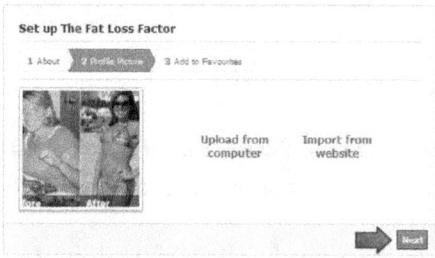

You'll now be prompted to add your new page to your list of Favourites on your Facebook profile.

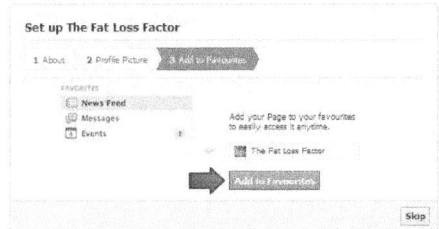

Congratulations! You've just set up your new Facebook Page!

There are a few things you'll be prompted to do. Firstly, Facebook will prompt you to 'Like' your page (see image below). It is a good idea to do this.

Remember, the purpose of your page is to get as much traffic to it, so that visitors will click on your affiliate link and check out the product you're promoting. The more people that 'Like' your page, the more traffic you will get.

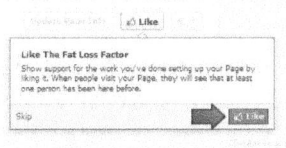

Next, you will be prompted to invite people to your page. We won't do that just yet because we need to add a little content first. Click '**Next**' to skip this step.

And here it is in all its glory... your Facebook Page!

Notice how your affiliate link is right at the top of the page in the Description :)

Just below the Description is a section where you can add new content. On Facebook Pages it is called a 'Status'.

Let's copy and paste the same thing we have in our Description into our status (see image below).

As you do this, Facebook automatically goes to the site where your affiliate link leads to and pulls pictures from the page to display in your status. You can scroll through the images until you find the one you're happiest with. You don't have to display an image with your status, but I recommend that you do. It will make your status post stand out so much more.

Once you're ready, click on '**Post**' to make your status live for all to see.

You can add as many statuses as you want, whenever you like. However, as you add new posts, the previous ones get pushed down the page, to make way for the new ones.

We want the post we have just created to be at the top of the page always. You can do this by selecting the '**Pin to Top**' option (see image below).

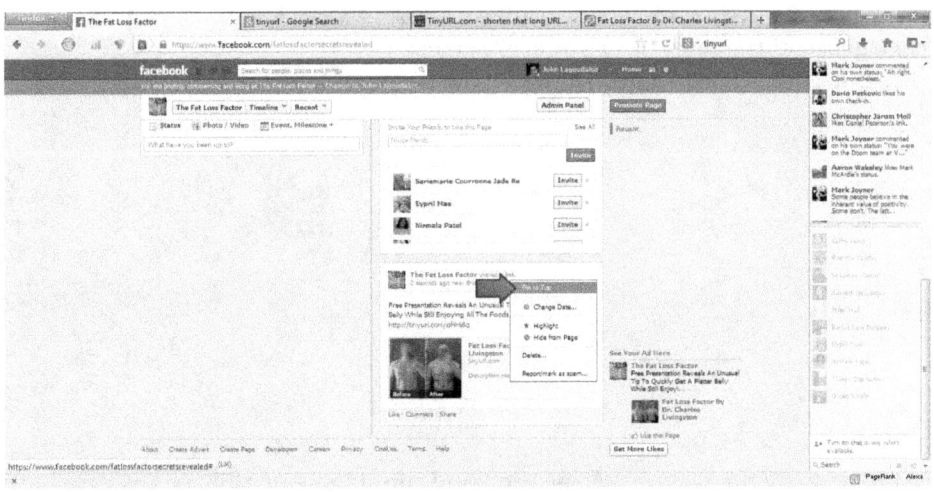

If you've done this successfully, you will see an orange ribbon on the top right-hand corner of your status post.

Now we are ready to start inviting friends to our new page. There will be a section on your page where you can easily invite your friends to 'Like' your page (see image below). Remember, the more Likes you get, the more exposure your page gets and the more sales you will make.

Now that your Facebook Page is up and running, your affiliate links are in the right places and you've invited your friends, you'll want to give people a reason to visit your page and share it with others.

You can do this by adding great content to your page on a regular basis. Content that is relevant to the product you're promoting.

The more interesting, or 'buzz worthy' you can make your content, the more visitors you will get to your page and the more sales you will make.

By adding content, I don't necessarily mean you will have to come up with advice, tips and articles all by yourself. You can do that if you know a lot about the topic and are passionate about it, but you can also post interesting articles, pictures, videos, links to websites, etc that you find anywhere online.

At every opportunity you get, encourage your fans (fans are people that have Liked your page) to engage with you on the page. Encourage them to make comments and share what you've posted with others that they know and can benefit from it.

The more you can engage with your fans, the more successful you will be.

9 KINDLE PUBLISHING

In this chapter we are going to go over what Kindle Publishing is, and how you can take advantage of this amazing opportunity to promote your affiliate offers, and make a passive income stream at the same time... all for free!

What is Kindle Publishing?

Kindle Publishing is about making books available to the public in digital format. These digital books are commonly referred to as ebooks. Ebooks can be read on your computer, tablet, smart phone, or electronic readers such as the Kindle.

Why take advantage of Kindle Publishing?

More and more people today prefer to buy ebooks over paper books. Why?

- Here are some important reasons:
- Ebooks are easier to access
- Immediate download

- Cheaper
- You can hold thousands of ebooks on one small device
- Little to no overheads for publishers!

Look at what's happening in the United States and in the U.K...

Ebook Sales Surpass Hardcover
for First Time in U.S.

Lauren Indvik · Jun 10, 2012

Kindle ebook sales have overtaken
Amazon print sales, says book seller
For every 100 hardback and paperback books it sells on its UK
site, 114 ebooks are downloaded in 'reading renaissance'

Shiv Malik
The Guardian, Monday 6 August 2012
Jump to comments (200)

This graph shows just how quickly ebooks sales are growing worldwide:

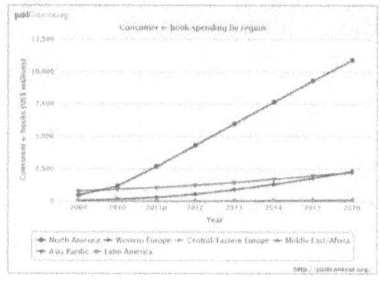

How do you fit in as an affiliate?

Kindle Publishing is like the holy grail for affiliates. Anyone can sign up for a Kindle Publishing account for free and you are allowed to publish any content you like for free. Yes, that's right; there are no fees at all to publish.

This means that you can write a report on your niche, or even a full-blown book if you are inclined and have the knowledge (or outsource it) and upload it to the Kindle marketplace. Now, within that report or ebook you can put your affiliate link ANYWHERE you like.

For example, you can put your affiliate link right on the inside of the front cover so it's the first thing that people see when they read your report. You can also put your affiliate link throughout your report and/or at the end.

My recommendation is to not make it look spammy or out of place. Put your affiliate link in strategic places that make sense to the reader.

Tip: Have your affiliate link appear in the first few pages of your ebook. Amazon allows anyone to take a 'Look Inside' the first few pages of every ebook. If your affiliate link is on one of those pages, you will get more people seeing it, which means more traffic to your affiliate offer.

Here's what it looks like when someone clicks to 'Look Inside' (see below). In this example, I have my website link right there on the first inside page. You can do the same with your affiliate links!

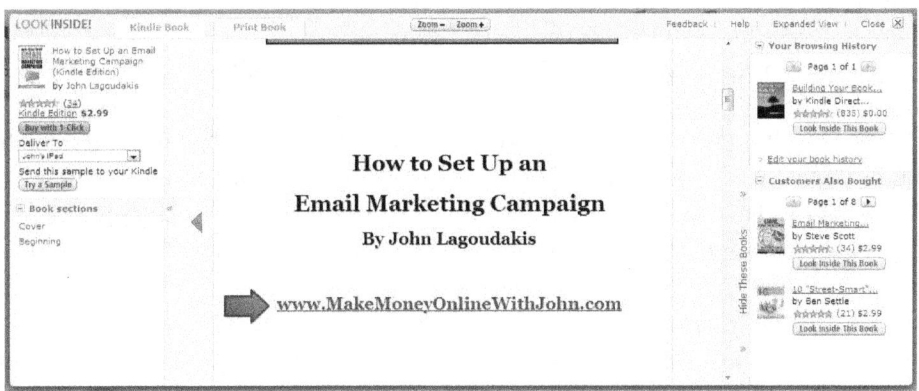

Another reason why Kindle publishing is a goldmine for affiliate marketers is that the people that go to Amazon's site are all BUYERS. They are not freebie seekers. These are people that are willing to spend money. This is the highest quality traffic out there.

What should I write about?

When thinking about what topic you could write about, I recommend that you take a look on the Kindle ebook store to see what the top-selling books are in your niche.

For the example of The Fat Loss Factor, we would go to the Weight Loss section of the Kindle eBook store and see what titles are the most popular.

Also, any report or book that has a 'Top 10' list does well. E.g. "Top 10 Ways to Lose 20lbs Within 12 Weeks".

Now, you can write your report or book yourself if you're passionate about your niche and have the knowledge. Other options are:

Research, collect notes and write your own content

Record an interview with an expert on the topic and transcribe the recording

Your content does not have to be long at all, so don't be overwhelmed! It can even be a one-page report. The important thing is that the quality of the content. The better the quality, the more exposure you will get.

What is the process of publishing your content on Kindle?

Amazon has created a step-by-step guide that reveals everything you need to know to get your content from your word processor to being published on the Kindle store. This guide is called 'Building Your Book for Kindle' and can be downloaded here for free on the Kindle store:

http://www.amazon.com/dp/B007URVZJ6

And here is the PDF downloadable version:

http://g-ecx.images-amazon.com/images/G/01/digital/otp/help/Building-Your-Book-for-Kindle.pdf

As you go over this guide, you'll see just how very easy it is to get your content ready to be published on Kindle.

How to make more sales

Once you've got your content published on Kindle (with your affiliate links in there - don't forget!), it's now time to promote your ebook to get as many visitors as possible. Yes, you will get some natural traffic just by virtue of being in the Kindle store, but there's one thing in particular you can do to really make a big difference in how popular your ebook is.

Get as many reviews for your ebook as possible.

The more reviews the better.

Here's why... Kindle buyers like to read reviews before doing anything. If your ebook doesn't have any reviews, it's going to be hard to get anyone's serious attention.

An easy solution to this is to ask family members, friends, etc, just about everyone you know to do you a big favour and head on over to your Kindle ebook listing and write a review for you.

Now, you need to be careful here. Amazon guards the integrity of their review system fiercely. Therefore, don't ask anyone to just go and leave you a positive review. It doesn't work that way. Do this instead...

Give your family and friends a copy of your ebook, ask them to read it, and leave an honest review for you at Amazon. That's it!

If your content is good (as it should be), you will have at least a few great reviews and this will really help you to get much more exposure... and make more sales!

Remember, the more reviews you can get, the better.

One other important thing you should do is to take the time to write a really compelling Book Description. When you're submitting your book to be published on the Kindle store, you will be asked to write up a Book Description.

In your Book Description, let the reader know what they will get out of reading your book (e.g. solve a problem, excitement, etc). You want to make them desperate to read your book.

You can also include testimonials or awards (if you have any) in your Book Description.

Extra bonus - Passive income with Kindle ebook sales!

Besides being a great way to get free, targeted visitors to your affiliate offers, Kindle publishing is also a fantastic passive income opportunity!

When you publish your content to Kindle, you can set whatever price you like for it to sell in the marketplace... and you get to keep most of the profits. Amazon takes a percentage of every sale, which is usually 30%.

This is an awesome deal considering that they provide a high-traffic marketplace, search engine and free advertising, they process all the sales for you, give you 70% commission on every sale, provide download access for the buyer, take care of any refund requests, and send you your check every single month like clockwork.

It's totally passive income... and at the same time, totally passive traffic to your affiliate offers!

Other marketplaces where you can publish your ebooks

There are other ebook marketplaces but we've only focused on the Amazon Kindle store because it is by far the most popular. You can also choose to publish your ebook on these other stores for even greater exposure:

- Sony eBooks
- Barnes & Noble
- Apple iBookstore

This brings us to the end of Kindle publishing.

In the last three chapters we've talked about three different ways you can drive traffic to your affiliate offers. While there are a lot of free ways to drive traffic to your affiliate offers, I've chosen these three on purpose for the following four reasons:

1. Long Term Traffic

Whenever you upload a video to YouTube, gain a new follower on Facebook, or publish an ebook on Kindle, that will bring you in traffic for YEARS to come.

2. Passive Traffic

What I love about YouTube, Facebook and Kindle ebooks is that they will bring you in traffic on total autopilot. Yes, even while you're sleeping!

3. Scale Your Traffic

It's simple really. The more videos you create and upload, the more followers you get, and the more Kindle ebooks you publish, the more traffic you will get. And you can grab as much of it as you like.

4. Highly Targeted

The people that find your videos on YouTube, your Facebook page and your Kindle ebooks, are those that have a great interest in that topic. There are no tire kickers here! These visitors are all super keen and motivated.

In the next chapter I get into other free traffic sources there are out there, but before I do that, let me stress as much as I can that these first three free traffic sources that we've gone over are by far the best, i.e. YouTube, Facebook and Kindle Publishing.

This is where you should focus most of your efforts.

10 OTHER FREE TRAFFIC SOURCES

Okay, let's say you're well on your way to creating lots of great videos for YouTube, you're adding regular posts to your Facebook page and you're creating content for Kindle AND you still have time to get more traffic to your affiliate offers, then here's a couple of other free traffic strategies you might want to try out...

1. Forums

Forums are online communities where you can discuss your favourite topics with others that share the same passion. Some forums are extremely popular and have thousands of active members.

The key to getting traffic to your affiliate offers from forums is to help people. The more you can participate in the forum and help out others with their questions, the more they will come to know you, like you and trust you.

You might be asking yourself, "How does this help me get more traffic to my affiliate offers?" It's very simple.

Most forums allow you to have a 'signature' (see next image). In the signature below you can see the person's name, and then a url. This is where you would put your affiliate link.

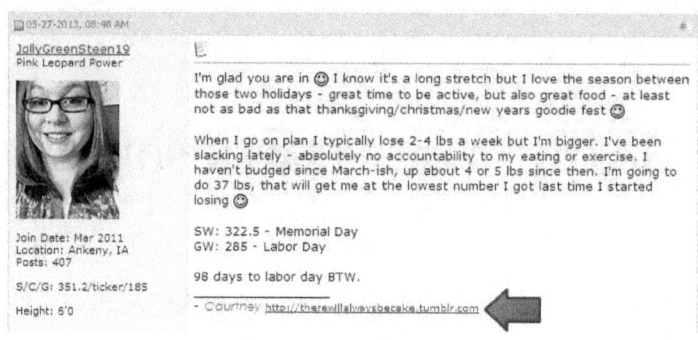

Just like an email signature, a forum signature appears at the bottom of every post you make on the forum.

When creating your forum signature, I'd recommend that you put a call to action before your affiliate link, e.g. "CLICK HERE to discover an UNUSUAL tip to quickly get a flatter belly WHILE still enjoying all the foods you love! - http://tinyurl.com/qf4r68q"

2. Guest Blogging

One way that I get lots of free traffic is blogging, but as this book is about how to have a successful Internet business without spending any money, I have left out setting up your own blog. Yes, it may not be expensive at all to set up your own blog (the cost is about $10 per month for a domain name and web hosting), yet it DOES cost money so it's not included here.

But there IS something you can do to tap into the targeted traffic potential of blogs and that is to write guest blog posts for popular blogs!

What is a guest blog post?

A guest blog post is where you offer an article to a blogger for him/her to publish on their blog.

Bloggers, especially successful ones, understand the importance of fresh, unique content for their blogs. This means that if you were to approach a successful blogger and offer to write an article for them, they would usually be happy to publish in on their blog.

They also understand that you would want something back in return, so they are happy for you to have a link in the article, pointing to your affiliate offer.

Here are the secrets behind getting the most traffic and sales from guest blogging:

- Approach blogs that already have guests posts

- Go for the blogs that get a LOT of traffic

- Provide quality content

- Don't be 'spammy' when promoting your affiliate link

Let's go into a little detail into these points...

Approach blogs that already have guest posts

It makes sense that blogs that already have guest posts on them are going to be receptive to your offer to write for them. Here are some sites that you can quickly and easily find blogs that want guest posts:

My Blog Guest - http://myblogguest.com/

Guest Blogging Tactics - http://www.guestbloggingtactics.com/blogs-that-accept-guest-posts/

Bloggers Passion - http://bloggerspassion.com/list-of-100-plus-blogs-that-allows-guest-blogging/

If you need help finding more blogs that you could approach, I recommend that you go to Technorati (http://www.technorati.com). Technorati is a blog search engine that lists the most popular blogs online.

Once you're at Technorati, select 'Blogs' from the search bar and type in a simple phrase for the type of blog you're looking for (see image below).

You'll then be presented with a list of blogs that are relevant to your search phrase.

Only approach blogs that get a LOT of traffic

Only offer to write a guest blog post on blogs that get a lot of traffic. It takes you the same amount of time to write an article and to approach a blogger to get your article published by them, so make sure you get the most out of your efforts!

There's an easy way to know if a blog gets a lot of traffic. Find out the blog's Alexa ranking.

Alexa.com is a free service that gives you the overall traffic rank of most websites. If a site doesn't have an Alexa ranking it means that that particular site hardly gets any traffic at all.

The lower the ranking, the higher the amount of traffic a site gets. For example, right now Facebook.com is the second most visited site in the world and has an Alexa ranking of 2. Wikipedia.com is the sixth most visited site in the world and has an Alexa ranking of 6.

To check a blog's Alexa ranking, go to http://www.alexa.com, type in the website url in the field provided and click on the green search button (see image below).

Alexa will return with some statistics, including its Traffic Rank (see below).

I'd recommend that you target blogs that have Alexa rankings less than 120,000. The lower the ranking the better.

Provide quality content

This sort of goes without saying at this point of the book :) Everything you write should be of the best quality you can make it. The better the quality, the more trust you develop and the more likely people are going to follow through on your recommendations, i.e. check out your affiliate offer.

Don't be 'spammy' when promoting your affiliate link

Don't go plastering your affiliate link throughout your blog article. It looks tacky and desperate. Also, the blog owner will be less likely to publish your article.

The acceptable method is to wait until the end of the article to promote your link.

CONCLUSION

Hey! You've made it to the end of this book. Congratulations! You've now learned everything you need to know to build up a successful Internet business from scratch with no money down!

The strategies in this book work. But just knowing this information is not going to make any money for you. You need to set yourself a plan of action and get started today!

A very powerful action strategy that I learnt a while back was to spend just 15 minutes a day on accomplishing a specific goal. If you're struggling with time, or maybe struggling to motivate yourself to take action, I highly recommend trying it.

Simply tell yourself that you will spend 15 minutes a day working on your Internet business. That's all.

On your first day you might sign up for your free Clickbank account.

On day two you might write down a list of topics that you're passionate about and choose one to work with.

On day three you might research that niche in the Clickbank marketplace to see if there are any products there worth promoting.

And so on.

By spending just 15 minutes a day working on your business, you'll be surprised just how much you can accomplish in a very short period of time.

It's all about taking action.

And let me give you a little tip... you will usually spend more than just 15 minutes a day once you get started. But getting started can be the hardest part, so tell yourself you only need to spend 15 minutes on it each day.

To Your Success,

John Lagoudakis

ABOUT THE AUTHOR

John Lagoudakis was born in Sydney, Australia and has been living in Brisbane since 2002. At the age of 31 he was given a copy of Robert Kiyosaki's bestseller book, 'Rich Dad, Poor Dad'. This changed the way John looked at money forever.

While working on different passive income opportunities, in 2007 John discovered affiliate marketing. He decided to give it a go and had a little success immediately. After that he was hooked. Recognizing the potential, he worked hard on his affiliate marketing business for 9 months and by that time was able to quit his full-time job forever. Less than 2 years later, he was one of the top 100 Clickbank affiliates worldwide.

Even in his early years online, John has shared what has worked with him with others. Today, John continues to teach thousands how he earns a full-time income online and is especially passionate about set-and-forget, passive income systems.

OTHER BOOKS WRITTEN BY JOHN LAGOUDAKIS

How to Set Up an Email Marketing Campaign

www.ingramcontent.com/pod-product-compliance
Lightning Source LLC
Chambersburg PA
CBHW071609170526
45166CB00003B/1034